W9-BGC-956

Spartans

by Paul Dinzeo

BELLWETHER MEDIA · MINNEAPOLIS, MN

Are you ready to take it to the extreme?
Torque books thrust you into the action-packed world
of sports, vehicles, mystery, and adventure. These books
may include dirt, smoke, fire, and dangerous stunts.
Warning: read at your own risk.

Library of Congress Cataloging-in-Publication Data

Dinzeo, Paul.
 Spartans / by Paul Dinzeo.
      p. cm. -- (Torque: history's greatest warriors)
 Includes bibliographical references and index.
 Summary: "Engaging images accompany information about Spartans. The combination of high-interest
subject matter and light text is intended for students in grades 3 through 7"--Provided by publisher.
 ISBN 978-1-60014-749-4 (hardcover : alk. paper)
 1. Sparta (Extinct city)--History, Military--Juvenile literature. 2. Soldiers--Greece--Sparta (Extinct city)--
Juvenile literature. I. Title.
 DF261.S8D57 2012
 938'.9--dc23   2011029087

This edition first published in 2012 by Bellwether Media, Inc.

Printed in the United States of America, North Mankato, MN.

010112   1202

Contents

Who Were the Spartans?

The Greek **city-state** of Sparta was one of the greatest military powers in ancient Greece. Spartan men spent most of their time training for war. They valued strength, skill, and bravery. Their courage and **discipline** struck fear in their enemies.

Spartan Fact

Many Greek city-states were surrounded by walls. Sparta was not. Spartans thought of their warriors as their wall.

Sparta rose to power about 3,000 years ago. Warriors were free Spartan men called Spartiates. They had a lot of time to train because of the **class system** in Sparta. Other classes served under them and did daily tasks. The Perioikoi were a class of free people who brought special skills to Sparta. They were craftspeople and merchants. The Helots were slaves with no rights. They were the class that served Spartiates.

Spartan Fact

Many other Greek city-states felt Sparta gave its women too much power. Spartan women were allowed to own land and were the heads of their households.

Spartan Training

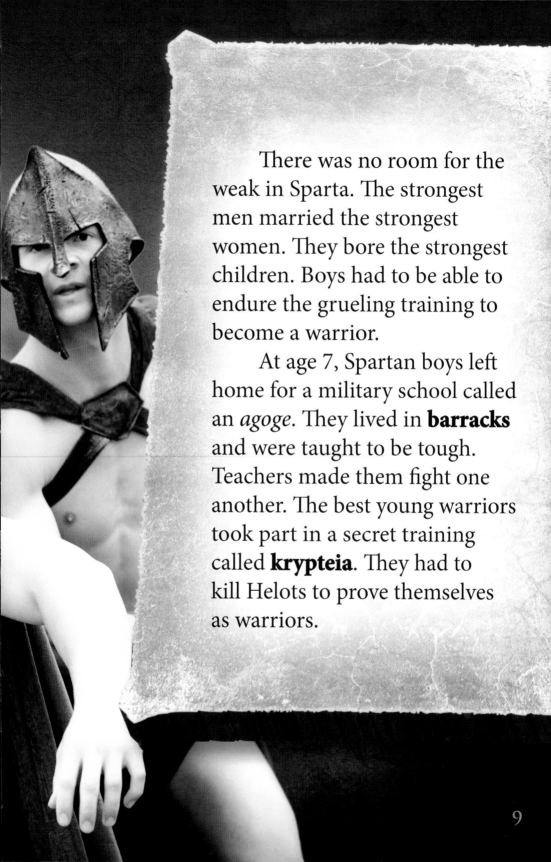

There was no room for the weak in Sparta. The strongest men married the strongest women. They bore the strongest children. Boys had to be able to endure the grueling training to become a warrior.

At age 7, Spartan boys left home for a military school called an *agoge*. They lived in **barracks** and were taught to be tough. Teachers made them fight one another. The best young warriors took part in a secret training called **krypteia**. They had to kill Helots to prove themselves as warriors.

Young Spartan men became soldiers when they were 20 years old. They served as full-time soldiers until they were 40 years old. They remained in the **reserves** until they were 60.

All Spartan soldiers learned to march in **formation**. The most famous formation was the **phalanx**. Soldiers marched close together holding spears and large shields. The shields overlapped to form a defensive wall. The phalanx was a powerful formation. Enemies needed huge numbers of soldiers to break through it.

Spartan Fact
The Greek word for a citizen-soldier was *hoplite*.

phalanx

11

Spartan Equipment

dory

The main weapon of a Spartan warrior was the *dory*. This spear measured 6 to 10 feet (2 to 3 meters) long. Spartan warriors also carried the *xiphos*. This short sword was about 24 inches (61 centimeters) long. It was often a last defense. A Spartan preferred to fight with his spear.

xiphos

hoplon

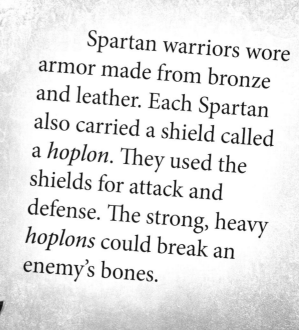

Spartan warriors wore armor made from bronze and leather. Each Spartan also carried a shield called a *hoplon*. They used the shields for attack and defense. The strong, heavy *hoplons* could break an enemy's bones.

Spartan Fact

Spartans were famous for their dark red tunics and cloaks. Red cloth was cheap and it hid wounds.

The Battle of Thermopylae

The Spartans fought the Battle of Thermopylae in 480 BCE. King Leonidas led a few hundred Spartans and their allies. Their mission was to keep the Persian Army from coming through a narrow mountain pass. The Persians may have had as many as 300,000 soldiers. Leonidas and his men held off the Persian Army for three days. Some believe they killed as many as 20,000 Persians.

Every Spartan died in the battle. Other Spartans later joined with more Greek forces to defeat the massive Persian Army in the Battle of Plataea.

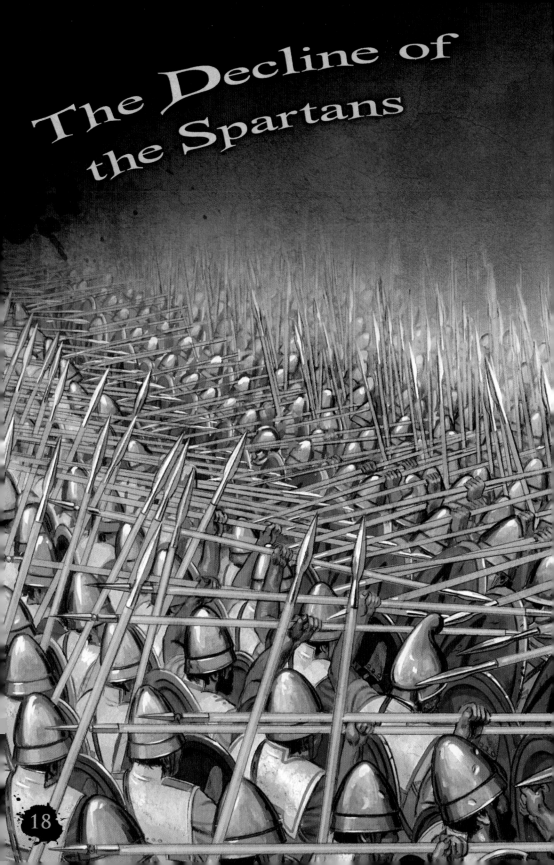

The Decline of the Spartans

The Spartans were almost always at war. These wars led to many Spartan deaths. The Spartans fought other Greek forces in the Battle of Leuctra in 371 BCE. Their enemies broke through the Spartan phalanx. It was the first time a full Spartan army had ever been defeated.

The loss at Leuctra was the start of a long decline for Sparta. Spartan citizens were greatly outnumbered by Helots and other classes. The Helots **revolted** soon after the battle. The Spartan way of life began to crumble. Sparta did not want to join with other Greek city-states. In 146 BCE, the Romans conquered Greece. Sparta fell, and its legendary warriors were no more.

Glossary

barracks—housing for soldiers

city-state—a city that governs itself and the surrounding area; Sparta, Athens, and Thebes are examples of ancient city-states.

class system—a social order based on status; people in a class system are treated according to their status.

discipline—order and control

formation—a set arrangement; Spartans marched and fough in formations.

krypteia—a secret training for young, skilled Spartans; young men were sent into the countryside to spy on and kill Helots.

phalanx—a military formation in which a large number of infantry troops march together, protected by a solid wall of shields

reserves—groups of military members who are not on active duty but can be called to fight

revolted—rose up and fought against

To Learn More

AT THE LIBRARY

Guillain, Charlotte. *Greek Warriors*. Chicago, Ill.:
Raintree, 2010.

McLeese, Don. *Spartans*. Vero Beach, Fla.: Rourke Pub., 2010.

Nardo, Don. *Warriors of Ancient Greece*. San Diego, Calif.:
Lucent Books, 2005.

ON THE WEB

Learning more about Spartans
is as easy as 1, 2, 3.

1. Go to www.factsurfer.com.

2. Enter "Spartans" into the search box.

3. Click the "Surf" button and you will see a list of
related Web sites.

With factsurfer.com, finding more information
is just a click away.

Index